Mindfulness

Dr Kimberley O'Brien

HODDER
EDUCATION
AN HACHETTE UK COMPANY

The Publishers would like to thank the following for permission to reproduce copyright material.

Photo credits

p.17 © kornnphoto/stock.adobe.com; **p.24** © David Marchal / Alamy Stock Photo

Every effort has been made to trace all copyright holders, but if any have been inadvertently overlooked, the Publishers will be pleased to make the necessary arrangements at the first opportunity.

Although every effort has been made to ensure that website addresses are correct at time of going to press, Hodder Education cannot be held responsible for the content of any website mentioned in this book. It is sometimes possible to find a relocated web page by typing in the address of the home page for a website in the URL window of your browser.

Hachette UK's policy is to use papers that are natural, renewable and recyclable products and made from wood grown in well-managed forests and other controlled sources. The logging and manufacturing processes are expected to conform to the environmental regulations of the country of origin.

Orders: please contact Bookpoint Ltd, 130 Park Drive, Milton Park, Abingdon, Oxon OX14 4SE. Telephone: +44 (0)1235 827827. Fax: +44 (0)1235 400401. Email education@bookpoint.co.uk Lines are open from 9 a.m. to 5 p.m., Monday to Saturday, with a 24-hour message answering service. You can also order through our website: www.hoddereducation.com

First published in 2020 by
Hodder Education,
An Hachette UK Company
Carmelite House
50 Victoria Embankment
London EC4Y 0DZ
www.hoddereducation.com

Impression number   10 9 8 7 6 5 4 3 2 1

Year   2024 2023 2022 2021 2020

Illustrations by Hannah McCafferey

Typeset in VAG Rounded 14/20pt by DC Graphic Design Limited

Printed in Spain

A catalogue record for this title is available from the British Library.

ISBN: 9781510481626

Contents

Mindfulness

Have you ever noticed what you're thinking, while you are thinking it? This might happen when you hear something new or smell something delicious. You might pause and listen harder, wondering, 'What is that sound?' or you might take a deep breath and try to guess, 'What's cooking?'

Mindfulness involves noticing our thoughts and feeling what our body is sensing while it is happening. Imagine you were moving carefully through a jungle, taking slow steps and listening to every movement in the trees around you. You would be aware of your thoughts and your heartbeat. This is being mindful.

On another day, you might be walking and talking without even thinking about where you are going or what is happening around you. Many people do this every day. If we do not practise mindfulness, we become less sensitive to our own senses and to the world around us.

Research has shown that it is important to be able to slow down and tune into our thoughts and senses. This helps us to develop greater focus. For example, many schools have found that when students practise focusing on the present moment for a few minutes in the morning or after lunch, they are calmer and more able to learn new information afterwards.

However, it takes practice to learn to sit quietly and relax, because the human mind likes to wander at first. The activities in this book will help you to think more deeply about mindfulness and your ability to focus on the present moment.

Let's get started!

1 Why give mindfulness a go?

Have you ever noticed that people can get really busy? We tend to rush and try to squeeze more things into our days. You might be asked to *move faster*, *hurry up* or *get ready*, from the moment you wake up until the moment you fall asleep.

Your brain is constantly processing new information, based on what you hear, smell, taste and feel. This can be tiring and overwhelming because your thoughts are always jumping from one thing to the next. You never have a chance to think deeply for a moment.

Practising mindfulness is about giving your body a chance to rest, without going to sleep. You can learn how to sit and settle yourself. This will improve your ability to focus and to absorb information more deeply. It does not take long – just a few minutes of regular practice each week!

What does mindfulness do?

✔ Sharpens your senses

✔ Helps you to focus for longer

✔ Helps you to feel more relaxed

✔ Helps you to sleep better

✔ Helps you to learn more

✔ Helps you to feel happier

✔ Helps you to appreciate the moment

✔ Helps you to feel less rushed

✔ Helps you to know yourself better

✔ Becomes easier with practice

▶ ACTIVITY ◀ Mindfulness words

You have started to learn about mindfulness. As you learn more about this topic, you will come across some new words. This wordsearch will help you to become more familiar with the new words in this book.

Find these words in the grid.

relaxation   meditation   focus   mindfulness

concentration   breathe   senses   aware

rest   recharge   emotional   clarity

C	H	G	U	R	S	L	K	M	N	R	R	E
W	O	R	G	K	L	E	B	N	U	E	R	E
M	I	N	D	F	U	L	N	E	S	S	S	T
E	O	K	C	E	L	M	N	S	I	T	R	R
D	A	L	R	E	M	N	D	T	E	K	E	M
I	R	A	D	C	N	S	I	B	H	S	L	M
T	W	A	F	H	U	T	H	R	Y	C	A	O
A	T	S	D	C	S	Y	R	E	H	L	X	U
T	E	M	O	T	I	O	N	A	L	A	A	J
I	R	F	C	U	V	H	R	T	T	R	T	H
O	R	S	S	L	B	E	U	H	U	I	I	A
N	R	E	C	H	A	R	G	E	K	T	O	R
O	N	C	N	A	E	H	M	O	L	Y	N	N

5

Now, let's start your mindfulness journey!

Take a moment to think about everything that has happened around you since you woke up. What have you heard? What have you seen, tasted and smelt?

Think about your feelings as well. Have you felt happy, sad or excited? What made you feel this way?

Notice the details

In a notebook, write or draw what you have noticed so far today.

Record what you have been thinking and doing.

Do not forget to include what you have been feeling. Use bullet points to make this easier.

Here is an example.

- Woke up
- Felt annoyed
- Remembered sports clothes
- Rushed to eat breakfast

▶ REFLECTION ◀

How did you get on?

Did you enjoy making a note of all your thoughts and feelings? What did you learn from this experience?

_____
_____
_____
_____
_____
_____
_____
_____
_____
_____
_____
_____

Why do we have random thoughts?

If a person's brain is healthy and active, there will be thoughts flowing through it all the time. According to the neuroscientist and philosopher Dr Deepak Chopra, humans have about 70,000 thoughts per day. That's slightly less than one thought per second. Does that sound about right to you?

Humans are like icebergs: there is a lot going on under the surface. As you look into a fridge, you might notice yourself thinking, 'What's for lunch?' But your brain will be busy thinking many other thoughts that you are not even aware of – for example, 'That cheese smells funny...', 'That light is bright...', 'Keep the door open but don't let the cold air out...', 'Don't waste power…'.

All these thoughts will rush through your mind and you probably won't even notice. These random thoughts help you to assess a situation.

Humans are very good at thinking and acting automatically. For example, when you avoid walking into a pole, the thought, 'Don't walk into that pole' will happen below the surface – in your ¦ subconscious ¦. You may not even notice you have thought about it: your body will just move to make sure you do not walk into the pole.

The thoughts you are aware of, such as, 'I need to buy my lunch', are called ¦ conscious ¦ thoughts.

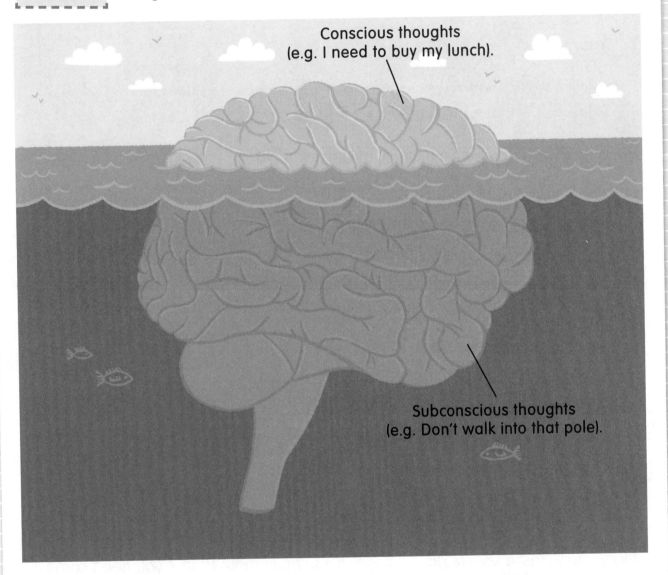

Conscious thoughts
(e.g. I need to buy my lunch).

Subconscious thoughts
(e.g. Don't walk into that pole).

Like an iceberg in the ocean, the human brain has more thoughts below the surface.

Step 1

First, take a guess. How busy is your mind? Give yourself a score out of 10.

10/10 is 'Super busy! I couldn't think or do another thing.'

1/10 is 'I feel really calm and focused.'

Your score: _____/10

Step 2

Next, answer these questions. Circle Yes or No.

1   Do you usually think about more than one thing at a time?   Yes   No
2   Do you try to do more things to fill up your time?   Yes   No
3   Do you aim to please people?   Yes   No
4   Do you have difficulty sleeping?   Yes   No
5   Do you avoid relaxing during the day?   Yes   No
6   Do you read less than you used to?   Yes   No
7   Do you struggle to remember things?   Yes   No
8   Do you write a 'To do list' most days?   Yes   No
9   Do you find it difficult to focus in class?   Yes   No
10 Do you dislike quiet time?   Yes   No

Step 3

How many 'Yes' answers do you have? If you have more than 7, you need some relaxation and you will definitely benefit from mindfulness activities. You are in the right place, so read on!

How many 'No' answers do you have? If you have more than 7, well done! You are taking care of yourself and you should not find it too difficult to sit, breathe and focus. This might be something you already do, but the activities in this book will give you more ideas about how to do it.

2 Finding focus and managing distractions

Focus is the ability to concentrate . Have you ever tried to focus and failed? If so, don't worry – it happens to everyone. For example, it can be difficult to do your homework in the kitchen while someone is cooking, especially if you are hungry. Or you might find it difficult to concentrate on what someone is saying if you can hear another conversation on the radio.

▶ ACTIVITY ◀ What do you like to focus on?

Most people like to focus on activities they enjoy. Sometimes, you will need to concentrate on a task you think you will not enjoy, like homework, because it needs to be finished on time.

In the boxes below, write or draw activities you like to focus on.

		Doing maths
Making a present		
	Writing neatly	

Why is focus important?

Focus allows humans to understand and remember new information. It helps us to see details more clearly.

When you see something new, your brain needs time to study it. You need to see clearly what it looks like and think about how things fit together.

Without focus, the information will not be clear. You will not see everything and you might fill the gaps with wrong guesses. For example, if you see an insect clearly, you will know it has 6 legs. If you do not see it clearly, you might guess it has 10 legs.

If the facts are not clear, your memory will also be unclear. You will have gaps in your knowledge. This can cause anxiety when you are trying to answer a question or remember something.

Step 1

Find a book and a timer or stopwatch.

Step 2

Start the timer and start reading your book. See how long you can read for before you check the timer.

Write down the time. This is how long you were able to focus.

Step 3

Reset the timer and start reading again. Keep reading for as long as possible without checking the timer.

When you do check the timer, write the time for your second attempt.

▶ REFLECTION ◀

1   How long were you able to focus?

1st attempt: _____ seconds / minutes

2nd attempt: _____ seconds / minutes

2   Did you manage to increase your focus?

Circle: Yes / No

3   If yes, what helped you to increase your focus?

_____

_____

If no, what made it difficult for you to focus and what could you do to fix this?

_____

_____

Well done! You are making great progress.

Step 1

Read about Omar.

In class, Omar sits next to his best friend, Nish. Nish loves to talk. He also likes to point to things around the room that he finds funny, like the wobbly fan above the teacher's head.

Omar has a lot of stationery. He likes to have all his pencils, erasers, sharpeners and glue sticks on his desk. Some things have toys attached to them or sparkles inside, so they are fun to play with.

Omar does not enjoy writing or drawing because his desk is missing a screw. It squeaks every time he presses down or moves his pen quickly.

Step 2

Write three things Omar could do to improve his focus.

1 _____

_____

_____

2 _____

_____

_____

3 _____

_____

_____

3 Meditation

Have you ever tried to think about nothing? Give it a go! Just close your eyes, take some deep breaths and see how long it takes before a new thought enters your mind. It will not be long.

It takes practice to slow down a busy brain, even for a few minutes! This practice is called **meditation**. It involves sitting quietly in a comfortable position, usually with your eyes closed, to give your body and mind a chance to **recharge**. Different thoughts will come and go as you gently breathe in and out.

Some people can sit and focus for longer than others and that is fine! The important thing is not how long you sit, but how you feel afterwards. Most people find they can think more clearly and they feel calmer when they open their eyes. Meditation is a way to refresh your focus.

If you found it difficult to meditate for the first time, you are not alone! Here are some responses from primary school children after they tried it for the first time.

Noises sounded louder. My breathing even felt like it was louder, maybe because my eyes were closed.

(Justine, aged 10)

All I could hear was people shuffling around, trying to get comfortable.

(Maya, aged 11)

I felt embarrassed and worried I might be seen by other kids walking past, or by anyone in my class who wasn't closing their eyes. But after about a minute, I just forgot about everyone.

(Tom, aged 12)

I kept thinking of things, like fixing up my scooter at my friend's house.

(Benji, aged 9)

Waiting for the timer to go off. That's all that was on my mind.

(Hunter, aged 9)

▶ ACTIVITY ◀ Can you meditate?

Follow these steps to get started.

Step 1

Choose a quiet place.

Step 2

Find a comfy cushion to sit on.

Step 3

Sit cross-legged or in a position that feels relaxed.

Step 4

Close your eyes.

Step 5

Breathe in slowly for a count of four.
Then breathe out slowly for a count of four.

Step 6

Check the time before you close your eyes. Check it again when you finish. See how long you meditated for.

Step 7

Allow yourself to relax a little more each day.

▶ REFLECTION ◀

Did these steps help you to meditate?

Where do you think you will find it easiest to meditate?

Sometimes, you will find yourself thinking the same thing over and over again. This is very common when you are worrying about something.

These thoughts are not helpful. They can distract you from other things, and make you feel miserable. However, there are things you can do to try to get rid of unhelpful thoughts.

How to get rid of an unhelpful thought

Dr Kimberley's top tips

✔ Notice the thought and accept it. Say to yourself, 'Thank you for that thought!' Do not simply pretend the thought is not there.

✔ Imagine receiving a message from your brain, to tell you it has received the thought.

✔ Imagine the thought is an unwanted knock at your front door. You do not have to answer the door. Instead, you can ignore the knock, or block the path to your door by locking the gate.

✔ If an unhelpful thought keeps coming back, you may need to give it some attention. Decide how much time you would like to give the thought (for example, 30 seconds, 5 minutes or 10 minutes). Set a timer and think about the thought for the set time.

Then, if the thought comes back, say to yourself, 'I have already given time to that thought. This is not the time.'

✔ Talk to a friend, parent, school counsellor or teacher about the thought. Talk for as long as you need to. Think about every possible angle until it feels resolved.

▶ ACTIVITY ◀ Stop the interruptions

Now it's time to practise!

The thought bubbles below show some unhelpful thoughts that could interrupt your meditation.

Write a sentence in each speech bubble to explain how you could let the unhelpful thought pass. Good luck!

Unhelpful thought
"I forgot to pack my lunch!"

What could you say to yourself?

_____

_____

_____

_____

_____

Unhelpful thought
"When is the timer going to go off?"

What could you say to yourself?

_____

_____

_____

_____

_____

Unhelpful thought
"What should I be thinking?"

What could you say to yourself?

_____

_____

_____

_____

_____

Group meditation

Did you know, meditation is often practised in classrooms to help students to concentrate and feel calmer? Some schools have been doing this for years. Others are beginning to try it for the first time.

Group activities – like learning a dance or a new song, or learning to meditate – are exciting! Meditation in class will work best after the excitement has died down, when everyone has settled. You will enjoy it more if you are relaxed.

Space is important. Give yourself and your classmates enough room, so you will not bump into each other.

Respect is also essential. The best way to show respect during meditation is to be as quiet as possible. This means you will not distract other people, so everyone will have a chance to enjoy the moment.

- Imagine yourself floating on water, like a leaf floating down a stream. You can feel the warm sun on your face. The water is very calm and your whole body feels light and relaxed.

- Squeeze your fingers into fists and tense your toes. Hold for 10 counts, then release. Breathe out as you let your fingers and toes relax.

- Next, squeeze the muscles in your legs and arms. Imagine each point of the starfish curling up, squeezing the water out of its arms and legs. Hold for 10 counts, then release. Shake out your arms and legs against the floor.

- Next, tense your stomach muscles. Make your tummy as hard as a rock. Hold for 10 counts, then release. Let your stomach relax and rub it with your hand, round and round in a circle.

- Finally, squeeze all the muscles in your face and head. Squeeze your eyes tightly closed and wrinkle your nose. Hold for 10 counts, then release.

- Use your hands to mess up your hair. Rub any lines from your forehead, or from around your eyes, nose and mouth.

- Let your whole body rest. Allow yourself to float. Breathe gently until you feel ready to roll onto your side. Then sleep.

Magic carpet

Imagine you are on a magic carpet and about to go for a ride!

Let your head fall back until you start to float towards the ceiling.

Now you are flying as free as a bird. Fly towards the ocean!

Feel the cool breeze in your hair and listen to the birds racing along beside you.

Settle back to Earth now. Relax for as long as you can. Roll over when you are ready.

Mind–body connections

Moving slowly into a position where your muscles feel stretched will help you to balance and hold the pose. Most people need to concentrate in order to stretch, balance and breathe at the same time.

These three simple activities – stretching, balancing and breathing – help us to remember the connection between our mind and our body. Sometimes, we are so busy thinking that we forget to exercise our bodies. Yoga is a popular activity designed to gently stretch all our different muscles in order.

Yoga poses

Would you like to practise some yoga positions?

Find a space where you can stretch out your arms and legs. Remember to move very slowly when attempting a yoga pose, so you do not hurt yourself. Yoga should not be painful or risky. It is a way to relax, so please take it easy.

Start with the easy moves first.

Circle the positions that feel most comfortable for you.

Cross out the ones you did not enjoy.

You can practise yoga alone or in a yoga class. Some people do a series of yoga poses every morning, called *Salute to the Sun*. Find out about some yoga routines.

Why not come up with a yoga routine of your own? It can be based on your favourite moves. What will you call it?

Draw your yoga routine below.

4 Your senses

Your **senses** help you to understand the world and survive in it. Humans have five basic senses:

- touch

- sight

- hearing

- smell

- taste.

Sensory stimulation makes life more interesting and gives us energy. Most people enjoy engaging their senses – for example, by listening to music, tasting chocolate or smelling something sweet.

Using your senses is also important for your mental health and physical wellbeing. If you have ever tried to keep an animal in a small box, or an insect in a jar with a lid, you will know it soon begins to look sick and unhappy. The same thing would happen to you if you were kept in a small space with no light and nothing to do.

Imagine eating a slice of pizza after weeks of eating bland, tasteless food. It would feel like an explosion of taste. Or imagine using your tablet or games console for the first time after being banned for a week – it would be super stimulating!

▶ ACTIVITY ◀ Sharpen your senses

These games will give you a chance to focus on each of your senses in turn. To really understand how special your senses are, it is helpful to stop using one sense and really concentrate on another.

To sharpen one sense, we need to limit our other senses. For example, wearing a blindfold limits our ability to see. This may allow us to listen more carefully or to taste more flavours.

Try being mindful with your senses. This is when you slowly absorb one sound, one sight, one texture or one smell at a time, moment by moment. This gives you time to explore each sensory input in detail.

In our daily lives, we rarely give ourselves this opportunity. So, give these exercises a try!

Sound

Sit beside an open window or on a balcony. Blindfold yourself.

Listen to all the different sounds you can hear. Can you tell what each sound is? Can you tell where the sounds are coming from?

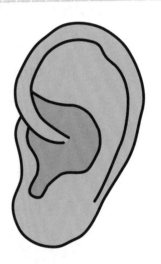

Sight

Stare at a garden or a busy street scene from a distance. Put on some headphones or cover your ears so you cannot hear. Does this help you to see more visual details?

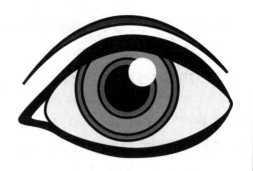

After three minutes, try to draw the scene from memory using coloured pencils.

Touch

Stand in a quiet place where you can feel a breeze. Close your eyes and try to feel the air on your skin.

Turn around slowly. Can you work out the direction of the wind?

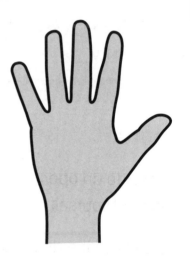

Taste

Close your eyes and place a tiny piece of food on your tongue. Allow it to dissolve slightly. Then roll it around in your mouth, slowly. Do not chew.

What textures and flavours can you feel and taste?

Smell

Go to a kitchen cupboard or garden and choose five very different items. Choose something fresh, like herbs. Choose something sweet, like a flower.

Let your nose lead you to the most interesting smells. What are you drawn to?

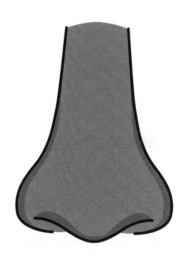

First, let's study the words we use to describe our senses!

Solve the clues to fill in the grid. All the words you need are listed below.

cover   focus   listen   overload   see

sensitive   smell   taste   touch   visual

Clues

Across

2 Look closely to _ _ _ the details.

3 The pie in the oven has a delicious _ _ _ _ _ _.

5 Soft music can help you to _ _ _ _ _ _.

6 _ _ _ _ _ the cat's fur to feel how soft it is.

8 I am _ _ _ _ _ _ _ _ _ to loud noises.

10 Colours and pictures are a form of _ _ _ _ _ _ stimulation.

Down

1 Put it in your mouth to _ _ _ _ _ the flavours.

4 When the birds start to chirp, I like to _ _ _ _ _ _ _.

7 Too much sensory input can feel like an _ _ _ _ _ _ _ _ _.

9 If the music is too loud, _ _ _ _ _ your ears.

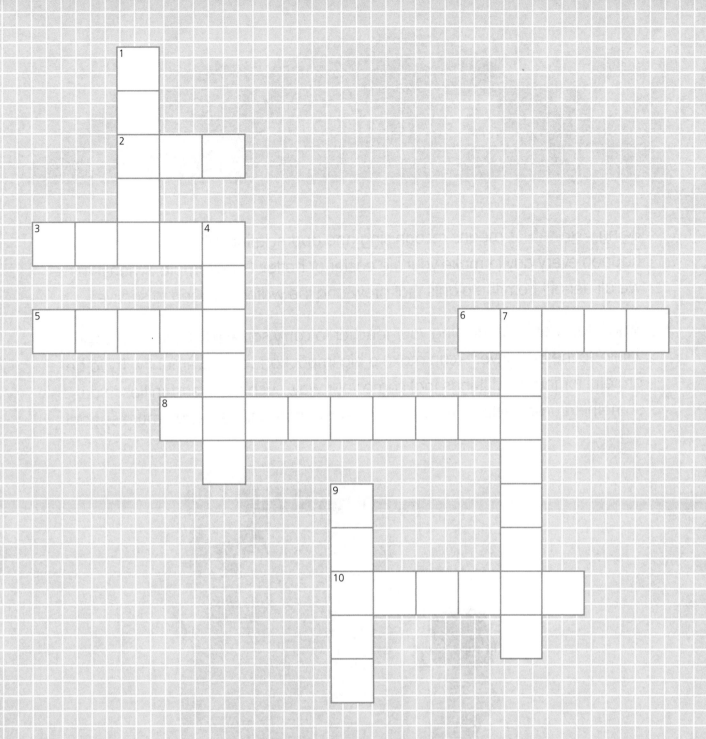

5 Gratitude

Being **grateful** means recognising and appreciating all the little things that happen every day to make your life easier or better. For example, when it rains, we all benefit from the plants that grow and the water we need to survive.

Small gestures – like helping your teacher to carry something heavy, or saying 'Hello' to the bus driver – can make a big impact on your community. Try to be grateful for the good things that come your way, such as opportunities to do something unexpected. This will make those moments feel even more special.

When we take time to notice all the small things we appreciate, it adds up to a lot of happiness and satisfaction. Being grateful every day is also good for our psychological health, because it means we release more **endorphins**. These are the hormones that trigger happiness.

Can you think of a few people who have said or done something you were grateful for? What could you do to thank them?

Step 1

In the table below, list five people or pets who have helped you in some way. Write what they did that made a difference.

Who could you thank?	What did they do?
My dog	He wagged his tail and made me laugh.
1	
2	
3	
4	
5	

Step 2

Share your list with a partner. Listen to what they appreciate.

Now, think of five creative ways to thank each person or pet on your list.

For example, your dog might appreciate a bone and you could bury it in the garden to add an extra element of surprise!

Write about or draw your ideas in the boxes below.

1

2

3

4

5

Some people keep a Gratitude Journal. This is a book where they write down all the special things they appreciate each day. For instance, you might write about the way your friend waits for you each morning before going to the playground.

You can do the same thing by writing the things you are grateful for on pieces of paper and posting them into a Gratitude Box. Why not make a Gratitude Box for your home or classroom?

Step 1

Find a cardboard box, like a shoe box or cereal box. You could also use a jar if you cannot find a box.

Make a slot in the top, like the one in a mailbox. This is where you will post your daily notes into the box.

Step 3

Step 2

Find the templates on pages 59–61. Use scissors to cut out the notes.

Invite your family or friends to use your Gratitude Box. Hand out the notes and pencils. Ask everyone to think of at least one thing they appreciated that day, or something they were grateful for. Then everyone posts their notes into the box. At the end of the week, you could read them out to each other.

You are getting the hang of being grateful. Let's try some role plays to practise.

Step 1

Choose one of these scenes to act out with a partner or small group:

- a new girl in dance class
- a missing school bag
- a lost child at the market.

In the boxes on pages 48–53, you will find more details to include in your role play. Each scene involves a random act of kindness, or something nice happening unexpectedly. Make costumes if you like and remember to have fun!

Step 2

The goal of each role play is to think of a creative way to thank the person who was helpful. You could use some of the ideas you see in the role plays to show gratitude in real life. Why not try these and see what happens?

A new girl in dance class

Kate is nervous about starting her new dance class. She walks into the room and it is full of older boys and girls. They all look very fit. They all seem to know each other.

One boy looks over at Kate. He points to a shelf next to the door. There are lots of boxes on the shelf, with water bottles and bags pushed into them. Kate realizes this must be where you put your things.

How could Kate show her gratitude to the friendly dancer?

Now, act it out!

Ask the audience

How else could Kate show gratitude for this act of kindness?

Write or draw your favourite idea below.

The missing school bag

Zeek is on the bus home. He is busy using his phone when he realizes the bus is almost at his stop. He jumps up and rushes down the aisle as the bus driver slams on the brakes. Zeek steps off the bus with his phone.

As the bus drives away, he realizes his school bag is not on his back. He has a terrible sinking feeling in his stomach. He cannot run after the bus now.

Zeek runs home to tell his older sister, Olivia, what happened. She asks Zeek for the name of the bus company. Then she calls their Lost and Found department.

The lady on the phone immediately contacts the driver of Zeek's bus. The driver checks that the bag is still on the bus. He says he is on his way back to the bus company. Olivia offers to drive Zeek to collect his bag straight away.

How could Zeek show his gratitude to Olivia?

Now, act it out!

Ask the audience

How else could Zeek show gratitude for this act of kindness?

Write or draw your favourite idea below.

A lost child at the market

Every Saturday, there is a huge market in Florence's town. People come to buy fresh vegetables and anything else their family needs. Florence and her two little brothers go into the market with their mother. Soon, they become separated in the crowds.

Florence cannot find her youngest brother. Her mother is walking ahead and does not realize he is not there. Florence stops to look for him, but then she cannot see her mother. She yells, 'Wait!' and she calls her brother's name.

A shopkeeper notices that Florence is upset. She offers to help: she lets Florence stand on top of a huge crate of watermelons. Now, Florence can see over the crowd. She spots her little brother ahead, with her mother – phew!

How could Florence show her gratitude to the shopkeeper?

Now, act it out!

Ask the audience

How else could Florence show gratitude for this act of kindness?

Write or draw your favourite idea below.

▶ ACTIVITY ◀ Surprise, surprise!

Coming up with a surprise can be lots of fun! Surprise parties are a good example of working as a team to celebrate someone special. Doing something special for someone is a good way of showing you are grateful to them.

Step 1

Discuss with a partner: How could you show gratitude together?

_____

_____

_____

Step 2

Discuss with your classmates: How could you show gratitude as a class?

_____

_____

_____

Who would you like to thank at your school?

Write about them or draw a picture here.

Glossary

Anxiety

A feeling of worry or unease. It might be about something in particular or it might be a general feeling.

Clarity

The feeling of everything being clear, so you can understand what is happening.

Concentrate

Keeping your mind and energy on one thing, without being distracted.

Conscious

Conscious thoughts are the ones you are aware of (such as, 'I need to buy my lunch').

Distraction

When you are in the middle of something important or enjoyable, and someone or something interrupts you.

Endorphins

The hormones that trigger happiness.

Focus

The ability to concentrate. Focus helps us to see details more clearly.

Grateful

Being grateful means recognizing and appreciating all the little things that happen every day to make your life easier or better.

Meditation

A practice to slow down a busy brain. It involves sitting quietly in a comfortable position, usually with your eyes closed, to give your body and mind a chance to recharge.

Mindfulness

Noticing your thoughts and feeling what your body is sensing while it is happening.

Progressive Muscle Relaxation (PMR)

A technique to relax your muscles, which helps you get to sleep.

Recharge

Bringing energy back into your body by doing something different or relaxing your mind.

Relax

Taking a rest from work or another activity to give your mind and body a break.

Senses

The ways in which you experience things. There are five basic senses: smell, sight, touch, hearing and taste.

Sensory stimulation

When something engages your senses. For example, a cake cooking in the kitchen will stimulate your sense of smell.

Subconscious

Subconscious thoughts happen below the surface. You are not aware of them.

Yoga

A popular activity designed to gently stretch all our different muscles in order.

▶ REFLECTiON ◀

What did you enjoy doing in this book? What will you continue to do in your life?

Templates

Notes for Activity on page 46

Cut out the cards below. ✂

Today, I appreciated _____ _____ _____ _____	Today, I appreciated _____ _____ _____ _____
Today, I appreciated _____ _____ _____ _____	Today, I appreciated _____ _____ _____ _____
Today, I appreciated _____ _____ _____ _____	Today, I appreciated _____ _____ _____ _____

Today, I appreciated

_____

_____

_____

_____

Today, I appreciated

_____

_____

_____

_____

Today, I appreciated

_____

_____

_____

_____

Today, I appreciated

_____

_____

_____

_____

Today, I appreciated

_____

_____

_____

_____

Today, I appreciated

_____

_____

_____

_____

Today, I appreciated

_____

_____

_____

_____

Today, I appreciated

_____

_____

_____

_____